BROKEN

The Rise of Radical Feminism

And the Decline of Western Civilization

©2017 K.Z.Howell

BROKEN

Introduction

What is feminism?

We have all heard the phrase, Radical Feminism, Militant Feminism, Third Wave Feminism. But just what is it and where does it come from? That is a far more difficult question than you would think. The roots of modern feminism actually pre-date the term and reach much farther back in history than most people understand. While many in the media and the current feminist movement would like for you to believe that they are a benevolent group of everyday housewives looking out for their own liberties, the truth is a much murkier tale.

True feminism, as Americans understand it, has not existed since the passage of the 19th Amendment in 1920. The Suffrage Movement, the women's right to vote campaign of the early 20th century, is considered the First Wave of feminism. In reality, that was the only wave. What the media and leftist politicians want you to call Second and Third wave feminism are very different organizations with very different goals. They are a creation of the movement and those behind it who have pursued a very different agenda for decades. Modern feminism is a tool to achieve a political and economic goal that has little to do with women's rights and everything to do with the downfall of capitalism, democracy and Western civilization.

Feminism has been made an ideology. Many of its modern supporters have no clue where their ideology came from or even what its end goals are for America. They only see the public face and hear the lip service that feeds whatever pet peeve the organization thinks will get voters or funding. As with any other ideology, Socialism, Communism or Islamism, the goal of Feminism is to perpetuate itself, It wants to spread its ideology in a quest for power, money and converts to its cause. That quest is never ending. As each supposed goal is reached it will simply move the goal and continue onward, victory can never be achieved because it can always make a new enemy to attack.

BROKEN

PART I

For the Detriment of Men and the Destruction of Mankind

No good thriller has a singular plotline. No good conspiracy has only one member. The real history of the feminist movement reads more like a James Bond script than a political and social movement. Modern feminism claims to have roots in the Suffragettes of the early 20th century, and that is a deceptive idea.

The modern incarnation of the women's rights movement goes back even further to the Socialist movement founded by Karl Marx and Frederick Engels in the late 19th century. The foundational principals of the Second wave women's rights movement came directly from the political theory of the European socialist revolution and the later Communist International (CommIntern) of Vladimir Lenin. While the majority of the socialist and even communist activity remained focused in Europe, a large and highly influential group formed in the United States in the late 1800's and began spreading the ideas of the socialist workers paradise across the American labor landscape. The deeply ingrained mistrust of European ideas by the American public and business community was not as receptive to the Socialist party's attempts to dismantle American capitalism as these early Marxists had hoped.

Early socialism in America focused primarily on men and the unionizing of American labor under the banner of socialism and with the idea of overthrowing the American republic through a workers revolution. They had used similar tactics across Europe to great effect and began their move here with every expectation of having like results. They received an unpleasant reception in much of America because America was not Europe. We had thrown off the yoke of the continental monarchal system many generations before and had tamed a vast landscape through the ideal of individualism and entrepreneurial spirit. The American men that socialism sought to bring to heel under the banner of Marxist collectivism had no trust in the European way and proved more difficult to intimidate than thought. While Marxist doctrine found strong support amongst intellectual elitists and migrant workers, most American showed little interest in giving up their freedom for the empty promise of collective bliss under socialist rule.

The Socialist Party of America struggled against this innate distrust of their message and paid dearly for every small victory. Their calls for massive labor revolts and violent factory takeovers were more often than not put down swiftly and harshly by either hired guards of the facilities or law enforcement. The SPA had great difficulty organizing large scale strikes across various industries at the same time not because they didn't have a plan, but because their plan was Eurocentric and relied on having a labor base of former serfs and illiterate peasants. America had had none of that for over a century and had in fact come out of a brutal and devastating civil war less than a generation prior. We wanted none of the strife that the socialists required.

Socialism needed a new plan. One that would allow them to grow in power and influence without drawing the ire of the authorities and the highly independent American men that socialism wanted to rule. Eventually they found a way.

Infiltrate and Emulate

Contrast the treatment of the various unionist and anti-capitalist movements of the late 19th and early 20th centuries with the Suffrage movement which occurred in the same era. Western women were accorded a far lighter hand by the authorities than the men's movements, some of which were put down with brutal efficiency when they began to spiral out of control. The typical male movement usually ended with bodies in the street and the sound of bone breaking. The women's protests were dealt with in a manner befitting the more traditional gender roles, despite some of the marches having small groups of socialist agitators seeded amongst the typical housewives and genuinely passionate activists. The very different handling of the women's rights movement versus the men's labor movement did not escape the scrutiny of attentive radicals.

That difference was not lost on the early Socialist Party of America and its various offshoots. Had they not been so busy fighting among themselves and paid more heed to the First Wave, they might have managed to co-opt the Suffragettes themselves and begun their takeover thirty years sooner. As it was, many of the most influential socialist thinkers and writers of the day recognized the potential and wrote extensively on how a women's movement could be used to bring down Western society and usher in a socialist utopia free of the bonds of marriage, parenthood and personal responsibility.

One of its most influential female thinkers was the writer, Charlotte Perkins Gilman. In her 1898 treatise, "Women and Economics" she advocates for the end of the "sexual economic relationship", her depiction of marriage. In her later works in the early 1900's she expands on her utopian ideal by basically engineering marriage, parenthood, personal property and individual freedom out of human relations and indeed out of engineering. Her work, especially "Women and Economics", "The Home" and "Human Work" read like an Orwellian nightmare and is a major influence on the theoretical basis for the entire Second and Third Wave feminist movements. Once the progressive/socialist party took over the Women's movement and coupled their agenda with it you can see the ideas of Gilman and others woven throughout the movement's personae.

Gilman's concept of a society without marriage, where men and women worked and lived as equals in communal housing and outsourced child rearing to a third party was the first serious blueprint of Vladimir Lenin and Leon Trotsky's socialist concepts that incorporated the complete dissolution of the family structure into a coherent economic and societal model in America. Her idea of such a society was widely celebrated amongst the academic's and social reformers of her time. Gilman's theories, along with the work of Russian immigrant and founding member of the Socialist Party of America, Antoinette Konikow, who advocated women's freedom from the class slavery of motherhood through contraception. The work and writings of Margaret Sanger on economic independence via birth control also did much to attract the attention of the Socialist Party of America and its affiliates in the growing women's movement in America.

Gilman, Konikow and Sanger and many other famous names were all active members of the Socialist Party or its union offshoots and celebrated supporters of the Suffrage movement. Sanger herself was an active participant in the Industrial Workers of the World (IWW) strike during the 1912 Lawrence textile strike which was among the first to fully utilize women as shields between the authorities and the socialist agitators to great effect. While the IWW itself was not a supporter of the Suffragists, its parent organization, the Socialist Party of America, was and many of its direct members and leaders were also staunch allies of this First wave movement along with their support for economic freedom for women through the Party controlled unions of the time. Sanger's dislike for many of the elitist organizers of the Suffragettes was based in the classism of the elites, not in the goals.

Many in the Socialist Party saw Suffrage as a separate issue to their aim of a Socialist economy and a distraction from legislative victories that would advance their cause directly. Others in the party saw the women's movement as a means of negating men's ability to overpower them at the polls and economically in the long term. This disagreement would eventually define the direction of later movements. Either way, the SPA felt that women's rights would be a powerful boon to the socialist cause, it would "thin" the vote by splitting man from wife and eventually would create a powerful and permanent voting bloc of women who were being convinced that their role in the family was no better than slavery. It appeared that the dreams of Marx, Engels, Lenin and Trotsky of a society wholly controlled and subjugated to the state could be accomplished. One of the main tenets of Socialism is the abolition of the family as the primary unit of society, with the expectation that the state would fill the role of mother, father and benefactor. These early socialist radicals had discovered the key to bringing Western civilization to its end and had they not misjudged the American psyche and our deeply held mistrust of European influence, they would have likely advanced their cause much more rapidly.

"To alter the position of woman at the root is possible only if all the conditions of social,

As World War One ended and the Suffrage movement wound down, the SPA's internal problems became more pronounced. The split between the radical action parts and those parts solely focused on gaining power through the slow process of subversion through legislation grew. Those that wanted to continue the push through direct action, labor agitation and violence squared off against the SPA elements that felt a longer view strategy would be less likely to be put down harshly by the authorities.

The overall Suffragist movement had had two distinct chapters that worked together hand in hand to achieve a singular goal. It's segregationist chapter and its non-segregated chapter continued the push for women's suffrage despite the differences. The issue of race and even the importance of suffrage itself helped tear the Socialist party in two. By the start of World War I, two main leaders of the socialist movement in America, Eugene Debs and Victor Berger, were already at odds over the issues of race and suffrage and the American entry into the war delivered the final blow. With infighting between the wings of the Party and a base torn by its own differing ideas on how to proceed, whether to support the women's movement, support for the war and racial issues, the party split in 1919 with many members joining the newly formed Third International , or Communist Party.

This essentially ended the Suffragist movement. They had won with the passage of the 19th amendment in 1919 and what is now called the First Wave quietly moved off of the front pages. Its organization, however, continued on with other aspects of the First Wave movement albeit with much less public attention to their activities. Many of the Suffragist movements' theorists and supporters from the socialist movement continued ahead with their own goals. With the split of the SPA and the defection of many of its members to the new Third International Communist Party, many of the SPA members didn't want to be with either. In the tumultuous period of the Roaring Twenties and the aftermath of WWI being the ascension of America to status as a world power, nationalism, capitalism and patriotism were renewed and the Socialist movement took a backseat. This unprecedented period of wealth and advancement ushered in a new political dynamic that created chaos among the two main American political parties as well. The industrial boom helped the Republicans, but the Democrat party went into flux. As it floundered in the early twenties many of the disaffected socialists and radical feminists saw an opportunity. Instead of switching to the Communist Party or remaining in the disfavored remnants of the SPA, they joined the Democrat party as Progressive Democrats.

It was from there that the seeds of destruction were sown. The First wave had effectively opened the door for many other socialist aims to be introduced into the American and Western European societies. Throughout the decades of the Great Depression, World War 2 and the postwar boom of the fifties, what were considered women's issues were used as wedge issues to further widen the rift between men and women. Slowly and steadily the progressive Democrats made inroads that were touted as furthering the liberty of women, but whose cumulative goal was the placement of political, academic and media surrogates into places of prominence. Many of the former SPA members and other socialist sympathizers quietly took positions in colleges and universities and advocated from the classroom. From these halls of academia came the journalists and politicians who now populate the news rooms, classrooms and halls of Congress. The end of the First wave heralded a new tactic from the left, the Long Game Insurgency.

BROKEN

PART II

The Rise of Radical Feminism and the Destruction of the Family

First wave feminism, the only wave of the western women's rights movement that actually sought to expand women's rights rather than limit men's or undermine society, saw its efforts bear fruit early in the 20th century. Through the efforts of organized women they brought about a more equitable and evenhanded legal standing that had been denied by tradition primarily and in some cases settled law. Women gained much in this period, the right to vote not least in the litany. In those early years traditional gender roles still held dominance in the economic and political arena. The suffrage movement was seen not as a threat per se, but more as an affront to many in the established political hierarchy. Men had managed to move Western civilization from horse and buggy to flight in less than fifty years, after all. Why fix something that wasn't broken?

In the end, women were granted the right to vote in the U.S. with the passage of the 19th Amendment. While they also gained much in the legal arena, later supporters of second wave feminism used the passage of the 19th Amendment as a whipping post for its own agenda. History has shown that the legal status gains of first wave feminism were far more important, and have had a much greater effect on women than simply the ability to negate her husband's vote. The ability to enter into contracts, equal parental rights and property rights were of far more importance to actual equality. Yet it was the right to vote that caught the attention of a growing socialist movement in America. It was at this time that many in the American Socialist movement changed their stripes and formed a new bloc within the traditionally conservative Democrat party and formed the progressive wing of the party we know today. One of the main reasons for the transition was the futility of trying to form a true socialist party in a country still inhabited and largely run, by traditionally conservative male capitalists. The socialists saw women's suffrage as a boon to their cause because they could now "split the vote" if they could convince women that whatever men wanted was always against the rights of women. In a brilliant game of subterfuge they began promoting other issues as being strictly women's issues in order to form a new and powerful voting base. Their efforts were somewhat blunted by the end of WWI and the ensuing economic boom that characterized the Roaring Twenties.

The Roaring Twenties did accelerate one aspect of socialist dogma that had been a subtext of the First Wave feminist movement. The moral fabric of American society changed dramatically during this period. Women moved out from the shadows of the booze and party underground and into the forefront of American popular culture. For the first time, female sexuality became an intrinsic part of popular culture, albeit in a form that today would raise no eyebrows. In the 1920's and 1930's though, it was considered borderline pornographic. The scantily clad vixens of the black and white silent picture and even the new "talkies" raised temperatures and the ire of many during its early years. The legalization and availability of birth control devices added a sense of acceptance to behavior that had before been deemed socially unacceptable. While everyone knew that loads of hanky panky were going on behind closed doors, the newfound sense of liberty among women and in the culture began to introduce a lowered sense of moral and traditional responsibility to younger and younger people, a trend that has never abated.

This political malaise for feminism as a political force, and a vehicle for socialism, continued through the 1920's and well into the 1940's. With the economic devastation of the Great Depression and the advent of WW2, America simply had better things to do than spend time and energy arguing over things that did not feed their children or secure the nation against tyranny. The family as the core of American life was still intact. Men and women still relied on each other when it counted. The bonds that had made western civilization an indomitable force against outside influence proved too deeply ingrained in human behavior to break. While the early leftists and their fledgling minority of radical feminists made few inroads during this period, they did identify the cornerstone of the "Nuclear Family" and began planning its demise.

On the legislative front, many of the basic tenets of socialism were mainstreamed through the ascension of former SPA members into the courts and congress. Several attempts to legislate away elements of the Bill of Rights and the American Constitution were tried, albeit with mixed success. Since America is a Republic any attempts at introducing socialist engineered programs required legislation. This both caused problems for the progressive/socialist agenda and gave it cover at the same time. One major tenet of early socialist thought was the imposition of state sponsored universal childcare. During the 1930's several bills were proffered that would have advanced that scheme on the federal level, including one that touted "24 hour free childcare 7 days a week" to "free the American woman from her burdens so that she might pursue the arts, a career or simply her leisure without the concerns of caring for her children". It did not make it very far into the process, the Great Depression was in full swing and there was no money to fund the program nor were there any "careers" for women to pursue.

The onset of World War 2 proved to be the biggest boost for this scheme, along with the mainstreaming of another major socialist goal, the flooding of the industrial workplace with new laborers. As men were conscripted into the military, women were rapidly pushed into every aspect of American industry. With vast numbers of men inducted and shipped overseas to fight Germany and Japan, women were forced into industry by the millions, even those that did not want to leave their children for the workplace. Rationing required many to gain employment just to feed their families.

It was during this period that Universal State Childcare saw its closest approach to reality. In order to keep women in the factories, State run childcare facilities were created to take care of the children in places where there were many industrial plants and high numbers of women were in the workforce. The progressive/socialist movement swiftly set about making the concept of women being in the industrial workplace, doing traditionally male jobs, hard labor, dangerous and health averse jobs, an appealing lifestyle for women through a propaganda campaign aimed at unionizing the women and advocating that they remain good workers for the state even after the war. Many women rejected the idea and remained at their jobs through a sense of national duty and patriotism, but as soon as the war ended, they threw down their rivet hammers and went home with their husbands and children. Despite the best efforts of the Marxist left, women were still women and the family was still the most important thing in their lives.

The period after WW2 and well into the "Baby Boom" of the fifties saw little action outside the bedrooms of a war weary and politically indifferent populace. It is this indifference that lead to the death of the American family as a binding force and created the environment that soon brought about the creation of the Western male as a second class citizen in his own home.

Second Wave feminism as a cohesive movement appeared around 1960. That doesn't mean that the radical feminists and their socialist allies had been dormant those many years. They had been very busy, working behind the scenes. It was during the lull of the 30's, 40's and 50's that they made their most important strides. For roughly three decades, the remnants of the Socialist Party of America had changed their stripes and greatly expanded the progressive wing of the Democrat party. The SPA had always advocated legislative victory over open conflict and they made good on their idea. Many former SPA members gained high offices in government, education and the press. From there, they advocated for more "rights" for women, occasionally tossing in a race related issue when it supported their aims. They pushed primarily for superior work rights for women over men and the general lowering of wages through flooding the business world with women workers.

Inroads were also made in the devaluation of marriage as a societal norm and the sanctity of family as the core of social, political and economic life in America as well as Western Europe. As the baby boom era of the fifties closed, a new left emerged from the socialized halls of academia. The work of Margaret Sanger had shifted from birth control as a means of timing families, to selective euthanasia as a means of <u>birth prevention</u>. Along with Konikow, the Russian activist, Sanger advocated the termination of pregnancy as a means of population control and the prevention of economic loss to the state through women leaving the workforce to care for children. The left's position became one of a choice between economic freedom for women to serve the state as worker bees, or enslavement in the household as a mother.

> *"...the peculiar character of mans domination over woman in the modern family, and the necessity as well as the manner of establishing real social equality between the two, will be brought out into full relief only when both are completely equal before the law. It will then become evident that the first premise for the emancipation of women is the <u>reintroduction of the entire female sex into public industry; and that this again demands that the quality possessed by the individual family of being the economic unit of society be abolished.</u>" (K. Marx, "The Communist Manifesto")*

Sanger's efforts to usher in a socialist utopia through sexual liberation from the evils of marriage and family via pregnancy prevention had failed to yield adequate results for the movement. Not enough women were abandoning the Judeo-Christian ethic in favor of the socialistic ideal of service to state above all others. When, in 1921, Sanger had founded the American Birth Control League, an organization that would later become Planned Parenthood, she was still the nation's leading advocate of birth control. Her conversion to negative eugenics occurred later when she became an advocate of legalizing abortion, especially among lower income African Americans. While Sanger's work was instrumental in mainstreaming the concept of abortion on demand, Planned Parenthood itself did not do them until 1970, 4 years after Margaret Sanger's death.

It is ironic that it was a woman who popularized the idea of a social engineering method even more brutal than the supposedly barbaric rite of the Spartans, who at least allowed the child to be born before deciding whether it deserved life.

Academia moves out of the classroom and begins its theoretical push in the streets of America during the late 50's as well. Noted authors and academic icons such as Saul Alinskey began to organize lower income neighborhoods all across the nation and founded myriad offshoot groups based on their theories of social justice. Alinskey is of particular note due to his ability to successfully organize and motivate people to seek changes in the streets through boycotts, sit-ins and large scale local and national protests. While Alinskey never joined any political party himself, his "Rules For Radicals" and his organizational system became, and remains, the basis for almost all community level organizing and indeed, even global movements.

Many of the anti-war movements of the sixties and seventies used his techniques to gain popularity among their target membership and to antagonize their opponents. After the publication of *"Rules For Radicals"* his popularity amongst the elite of the progressive Democrat party grew by leaps and bounds. He died only a year after the publication, but his legacy lives on through the many young politicians his work influenced and the admiration his offensive but often humorous protest methods engendered in his followers.

Just before his sudden death in June of 1972, Alinskey was planning his next organizing push. He intended to begin work on turning the white, middle class in America away from traditional conservative ideals and toward his ideal of anarcho-socialism. Many high ranking social and political figures such as Cesar Chavez, Hillary Rodham Clinton, Tom Gaudette and many others, credit Alinskey as a major influence, and his influence within academia cannot be overstated. The vast majority of the student movements and radical anti-war and anti-capitalist movements of the sixties and seventies are rooted in Alinskey's organizational doctrine. It is also Saul Alinskey's organizational technique and his tactics, codified in 1971 in "Rules For radicals", that inspired and ignited the 1960's Second Wave Feminist movement, especially the new version of radical feminist that emerged from the bra-burning, free love groups that the press splashed across the television screens of the period at every opportunity.

The Second wave had many influential men and women emerge in the early 1960's who had been heavily influenced by the socialist radicals of the first wave and the ensuing decades of the movement's relative obscurity in the public eye. The dawning years of "the age of Aquarius" saw the emergence of an American variation of the European socialist elite that based its political philosophy on a narrow interpretation of Marx and Engels *"The Origin of the Family, Private Property and the State"*. Published in 1884, *"Origin"* and its focus on the status of women under a communist ideal became the go to reference for many of the writers that became prominent voices in the 1940's, 50' and 60's. Despite having much of its source material in human social evolution refuted by later researchers, Marx and Engels basic concept of society and family remained a source of extrapolative thought for many adherents to the totalitarian ideal of a perfect social order.

"Origin" was primarily based on the work of anthropologist Lewis Henry Morgan, who in turn based his theories of social evolution on the structure of Native American society. The fallacy of equating industrialized societal structure on a primitive tribal, nomadic and mostly matriarchal culture that revolved around familial bloodlines is obvious in hindsight, but Morgan's

work was groundbreaking at the time. This scientific error was conveniently ignored by the socialist thinkers of later years in favor of further promulgating the myth of the oppressed female in modern society. The patriarchy and institutionalized misogyny is a necessary device for radical feminism and the devoted socialist. Reality is irrelevant to the cause, only the narrative matters.

From the tenets found in *"Origin"* the feminist writers developed a whole new take on male and female relations, always with an eye toward promoting the idea of men as little more than rapists and slaveholders and women as victims and an evilly oppressed underclass. In Europe, the work of Simone de Beauvoir was particularly well received in the feminist circles of her era in the late 40's and 50's. Her book, *"The Second Sex"*, spelled out the early version of what is now called the patriarchy and set many later feminists on a course of blaming all men for the perceived oppression of all women.

When Betty Friedan published her bestseller *"The Feminine Mystique"* in 1963 it was heavily influenced by de Beauvoir's *"The Second Sex"*, furthering the original socialist ideals that *"The Second Sex"* had taken from Marx and Engels tome. Friedan focused her book on the way mostly white women were addressed in the mainstream media. She wrote against the ideals the media promoted in shows like "Father Knows Best" that showed women as content, and happy mothers and homemakers. Her own polls of her former college classmates indicated, to her, a deep dissatisfaction with traditional family roles and from that she extrapolated that all women were oppressed by all men because women were not out in the workplace. Quite a leap based on a handful of college educated friends who lived insular lives in 1960's America.

While Friedan's *"The Feminine Mystique"* was making waves in the feminist ranks of American society, John F. Kennedy was busy making women's rights a keystone issue of his New Frontier program. Kennedy's *'Presidential Commission on the Status of Women'*, a blue ribbon cabinet level advisory board, studied women's issues and released their report in 1963. This report added fuel to the fire of feminism by acknowledging wage discrepancies and promoting paid maternity leave, among other findings. One takeaway from the early Friedan era should be the focus on creating a federally funded universal daycare system. Oddly reminiscent of the earlier attempts to create a parentless society.

As this new Second wave gained victories for women on their face, the creation of the Equal pay act, Title VII and the EEOC undermined the ability of companies to hire the most qualified applicants and eroded the wage and job security of millions of men. Each new victory against the mythical oppressive patriarchy moved federal and judicial power further toward totalitarianism towards males and weakened the American economy and society through endless regulations that no one could interpret.

Friedan went on to create the National Organization for Women and became its first president in 1966. The organization achieved many victories for women under her leadership. Friedan was pushed out of NOW in 1969. Ser insisted that middle and upper class women were more deserving of employment than poverty stricken African American males. Most of the NOW board disagreed and the feminist movement fractured. Ever more radicalized alternatives sprung up all over America, each with its own agenda and axe to grind but with the same theme of all men evil and socialism the only way out of patriarchal oppression for women.

While Betty Freidan was the political face of the early second wave, its social face was Gloria Steinem. Steinem rose to prominence after publishing her diaries from a stint undercover as a Playboy Bunny in 1963. Her incredible revelation, that cocktail waitresses were expected to part men from their money by encouraging them to buy booze, took the entire nation by surprise and propelled Steinem to feminist stardom that exists even now. If her elevation to the lofty heights of social revolution over the job description of a cocktail waitress proves anything, it is that feminism is no longer about raising up women. It had turned toward bringing down men. That trend has accelerated at a steady pace ever since.

On the legal front, Second wave Feminism and its cohorts in academia and the courts won many victories under the banner of supporting the ERA. In an epic game of cat and mouse, the focus of the nation was placed squarely on the Equal Rights Amendment, while the goals of the progressives were more along the lines of death of the family by a thousand cuts. A complicit news media, now run by former radicals and populated by journalists steeped in socialist values, distracted America with pictures and stories of bra burning and mass marches. But the real work was being conducted out of sight and off of the front page. In the period between 1963 and 1980 the Pill became widespread, abortion became commonplace, Title IX, Title VII and the EEOC drove millions of men from the workforce and closed thousands of businesses. Supposed feminists vanguarded the open borders policy, promoted teen and out of wedlock sex and directly increased the welfare state through its promotion of government as surrogate husband. Men only schools were forced out, men only clubs and fraternal organizations were pushed out of existence, all the while the feminists were demanding their own spaces, schools and accommodations among educational and military institutions. The hypocrisy of Second wave feminism came honestly, they were formed from progressive socialist ideals and under socialism some are always more equal than others. This tactic is straight out of Alinskey's playbook for overloading the system.

The one major setback for the socialist/feminist plans came in 1971. With America distracted by anti-war protests, free love sit-ins and the debate over ERA, congress had passed the Comprehensive Child Development Act. Despite the Acts benign name, it was designed as an entitlement on the scale of Medicaid and Social security combined. It would have mandated federally funded childcare that covered 100% of the families in America. It provided not only childcare, but education and medical care as well. The initial funding was to be $2 billion (that's $10 billion in today's dollars) but conditions were very different in 1971. America still controlled its borders then. Estimates for such coverage now with an estimated 8 million illegal alien children added to American children are as high as $90 billion per year now. President Nixon vetoed the measure and gave a scathing rebuke at the attempt to create a government run indoctrination scheme in the United States.

> *"Give me four years to teach the children and the seed I have sown will never be uprooted."*
> *(V. Lenin)*

Coverture.

A simple word. A small word. But a word with exceptional power within a family structure. It means "to cover" and in legal terms it meant that a husband and wife were one, even in the eyes of the law. This simple little legal fiction turned out to be the means by which the feminist/socialist alliance could bring down the last remnants of the Nuclear Family and render Western Men impotent to stop his own demise. In 1966 the U.S. Supreme court, in an opinion by Hugo Black, stated that coverture was an archaic remnant of a caste system, despite the fact that coverture had not subsumed women into the rights of the husband since the early thirties. The remains of coverture erased by the opinion were the legal fiction that prevented a spouse from cheating and still getting everything when the marriage dissolved. Coverture treated both the husband and the wife as a single entity. If a husband failed in his duties to her, she had standing in the eyes of the law. If the wife failed in hers, the husband had equal standing and the courts had to rule in that manner.

With the ink not even dry yet on Justice Black's opinion the feminists began their push for the ERA despite knowing it would never happen. The goal was to push for everything publicly with the ERA (which did nothing not already covered by existing law), and run a hearts and minds campaign based on the amendments opposition. The feminist/socialist alliance of Second wave feminism used the argument to radicalize more and more women and indeed, millions of men by proxy, into the counter culture movement of the sixties and early 70's. This movement had two main agenda's, its primary goal was to separate women from men and its secondary goal was to radicalize the education system to the point where the language could be controlled entirely by their own sympathizers. This tactic succeeded spectacularly, largely due to the Vietnam War and a press that wanted images and soundbytes for the evening news no matter the cost.

The deleterious effects of Black's opinion are still playing out today, but let's stay in the Second Wave era to maintain our timeline. With the last legal protection of the family now gone, the path was wide open to begin the destruction of the society built on the family unit. The long game played by the socialists coupled with the political immediacy of a feminist movement rapidly gaining steam and press coverage began to pay big dividends. The cabal's main agenda, the breaking of the bond between men and women, took root in the counterculture of the sixties and grew to ever more prominence through the mid to late seventies. Women were the focus and with a willing accomplice in the press they made major inroads into the very fabric of society.

The socialist activities were focused on the long game of politics but feminism pressed hard to rip apart the moral and religious foundations of society. Women were convinced by lies and exaggerations that they could do anything they wanted. They paid special attention to the younger generation of the time and convinced them that drugs, sex and freedom were their right by birth and that men were keeping the good life from them. They were taught that children were the shackles and abortion the key to their padlock. They pushed the mantra of men as an evil oppressor and that men especially were to blame for wars. American men. American business men to be exact. They laid no blame on communist expansion. In fact by the mid to late 70's they openly embraced Soviet doctrine as a model for women's rights despite the fact that communism was still the primary fear in America at that time. It was at this point where Second Wave feminism began to falter. Its adoption of the socialist mantra of men bad, communism good turned off many of its supporters.

While Second Wave feminism essentially died out by the early 1980's in the U.S. it continued overseas for years afterward. At roughly the same time period, the progressive (socialist) wing of the democrat party also saw a drastic change in its fortunes. Economic turmoil, Soviet expansionism and a general distrust of anything vaguely socialist pushed the movement into the background of politics, though its adherents remained in power and in positions of influence. The ignominious demise of the Second wave was too late though. The damage had been done. The American education system and the majority of the mainstream press were solidly in the hands of the feminist/socialist alliance. The long desired split between men and women was moving forward under its own steam now. Two generations of women were now convinced that men considered them no more than sexual chattel. Even the Reagan era of nationalism and traditional values could not undo the damage, and the rot of American society continued.

BROKEN

PART III

Third Wave Bedfellows and the Law of Unintended Consequences

A Movement In Search Of a Meaning

While the Second Wave feminist movement sought to abolish traditional marriage and change male/female moral and social codes, it also set in motion the decline of society by subterfuge. Both activities were wildly successful. With the Soviet Union in decline and a more patient, less overtly hostile progressive wing of Democrats now fully entrenched within the party, the decision was made to pull back from the feminist movement and concentrate on the new policy of political correctness. The resultant slow collapse of support for the Second Wave movement did two things to further the goals of the progressive apparatchik. First, it took the focus off of them and allowed them to continue their takeover of academia and the press from the shadows. The Reagan Era was a blessing to this tactic as it turned all eyes outward to the goal of a bloodless victory against communism and away from the activities of the socialist/progressive activities at home. The second boon was the creation of a massive organizational structure that the progressives used to great effect in spreading their ideology and sowing dissent even further into everyday family life. It was the leftover cadre of Second Wave feminists, the hardcore elements, that focused on destroying traditional, morality based society and the family structure.

The Second Wave had achieved its primary goal of "freeing" women from the remains of coverture and the supposed tyranny of marriage. I cannot stress enough how much damage that did. On its face, it allowed women a degree of personal freedom that had been supposedly denied them. The right to contract in their own name (which already existed in state law) it also freed women to start their own business (which already existed in state law), it allowed women to create debt in their own name without a husbands consent but using his income and standing. That last one was the sole remaining economic liberty that coverture still enforced in most states. That all sounds perfectly reasonable until we look a little deeper. The abolition of coverture also restricted the rights of a male with the same ink it used to supposedly free women. A husband no longer had what the law phrased as "the right to her labor". That's right gentlemen, once you say "I Do" your brand spanking new bride can literally sit on her ass and do absolutely nothing and you have no legal recourse to sue for divorce on the grounds of non-participation, but if you do the same your blushing bride can. The same goes for sex.

Prior to Hugo Black's Supreme Court opinion, men had a legal expectation of both an active partner in the household and in her "feminine charms". Absent those primary marital expectations a man could sue for divorce on those grounds and usually win. Until the death of coverture, husband and wife were considered one legal entity, one equal to the other in both rights and responsibilities. This aspect was last to fall because even the courts recognized that such a system was untenable and would lead to massive social upheaval. Just as intended, the remedy applied was the Soviet doctrine of the No Fault divorce. California led the way in 1969 as the first American state to model its family law on Soviet doctrine. By 2010 all states had adopted the Soviet model of No Fault divorce and the results were astoundingly similar in each one as the scheme was implemented. Within two years of adoption divorce rates, which had been steady for decades, surged 500%, women were forced into the workforce in ever higher numbers and female poverty soared.

I have spent a great deal of ink on the seemingly marginal importance of the legal fiction of coverture. I have done so because Third Wave Feminism did as well. It was a cornerstone of traditional marriage, and the ending of the family structure could not proceed with Western Men being equal partners in the family. The period between the slow dissolution of Second Wave feminism and the resurgence of what is now known as Radical Feminism, or

33

Third Wave feminism between roughly 1980 and 1990 was a tumultuous time in the courts. Even though women could create debt in their own name by law, the banks and retailers weren't stupid. The court had changed marital law, not contract law. A wife could now create debt based on marital resources without the husbands consent but under the law of contracts, coverture still existed. Men no longer had the right to disagree, but they did retain the legal responsibility for the debt the wife incurred. Women had gained the right to withhold sex, and were encouraged to use it as a bargaining chip and weapon against their husbands.

By this time the married couples were the same people who had been the counter culture libertines of the sixties and seventies. The seeds of promiscuity, drug use and the instant gratification mindset had been planted and popular culture was feeding its growth with abandon. "Womens Lib" became the catch phrase and popping pills and doing the pool boy while hubby was off working became the norm. All the while, the press lapdogs of the leftist cabal spewed an endless stream of derision and hatred for men into the airwaves and onto the pages of the newspapers and magazines. Television made marriage and family the laughingstock of nightly sitcoms and movies made infidelity and promiscuity an ideal to strive for not a moral lapse to avoid.

All the while, Third Wave feminism is building in the background. Western males still hold the economic and political high ground. The feminist/socialist alliance had pulled many blocks from the foundations of society but they simply didn't have the numbers and economic clout to finish off the men in the West once and for all.

By 1990 or so, the progressive wing of the Democrat party and its socialist allies in congress and the courts had successfully removed God from any aspect of public life to such a degree that in many places it had become criminal to display the Ten Commandments or a Christian cross in public. That trend still is in play in isolated areas to this day. There is no God in court or the schoolhouse any more. Western men built a civilization based on the moral and ethical tenets of Judeo-Christian thought and Third Wave Feminism was resurrected from the organizational system the progressives had used to take over academia and the press. With those goals solidly in hand, they now turned their attention to back to the ultimate prize. The Feminist Final solution for Western men.

Western man had obligingly assisted in his own demise throughout First and Second wave feminism but he still retained an overwhelming edge in economic and political power. Something had to be done to remove that last element or the progressives risked having Men rally and stand against their plans from a position of strength. Western Mans last power was inseparably tied to the middle class economic model that had made America and indeed, all of the West, the most powerful civilization in history. Many men still had their families despite the Feminist and socialist efforts to break that bond. We had survived intact almost exclusively in the flyover parts of America. While divorce and single parent households had become the norm in the socialist controlled regions, many areas of the rural states had yet to feel the full effect of the cabals attentions.

Somewhere around 1992 to 1994 they turned their eye toward us. Think back to the early 90's and into the early 00's. Every night on the news there was another lawsuit reported against a rural school district that had some vestige of God left on campus. Even the pre-game prayer became fodder for NBC, ABC and CBS and not just the local affiliates. The big city bureaus would do pieces on tiny little Nowhere, Nebraska because a coach knelt before every game. State legislatures from Florida to the Dakotas were dragged through a national wringer for not making million dollar accommodations to a public school district with one wheelchair bound student (often none) and an annual district budget of a half million. High schools and colleges were forced to pay billions for sports equity for females even when they had no female teams. Potty parity I'll concede. That was necessary.

How does all that tie in with third wave feminism? Remember what I said about the progressives keeping the Second Wave organization intact? When the Second Wave petered out in the Reagan era, the organization itself continued. It simply retasked to the academic and social shadow movement and continued to spread dissent and propaganda to women. They created a multifaceted organizational structure that grew slowly and seeded dozens of smaller movements throughout the political and social landscape. Seriously, you thought that lesbian single mom who sued the school district in Columbia, South Carolina had the juice to bring a billion dollar law firm to a county school board meeting? Yeah right! And pigs fly.

Throughout the 90's the Third Wave picked up steam and followers. They gained a great deal in the elite rich lady support from the coasts but they needed numbers. They got them from the many disparate groups they folded under their umbrella. Third Wave feminism barely even gives lip service to womens issues beyond cost free unlimited abortion on demand and legal superiority for women as an aside to their drive for legal superiority for anything that is not white, male and American. Third Wave feminism is the prime driver for open borders. Global citizenship, superior legal status for every LGBTQ, illegal alien, climate change believer, Jihadi, Islamist, social, economic, gender or socialist refugee they can find. This brings us to the latest ally of Third Wave feminism.

Islamists.

That's right. Those shining examples of tolerance and inclusion. Those turban wearing rascals of romanticism. Third Wave feminism has finally found the Holy Grail of women's issues and lovingly wrapped them up in their arms. Asking why is like asking a shark why it has teeth. They need allies for their next move and Islam provides the one thing they lacked, a well organized militant wing. Since Third Wave feminism can't stomach any hint of

37

traditional family values, as evidenced by their recent Women's March, they have chosen to ally with another traditional system. Shariah. Other than that pesky little bit about women being the chattel of Islamic men, the Third Wave acquires substantial funding and an instant army by allying with an Islamist movement that advocates global Shariah as a form of women's liberation. That their idea of liberation is slavery, child rape and life as property less valuable than a goat is irrelevant. Their unholy alliance is another example of the hubris of leftist thought. As the titular head of the so called Islamic Women's rights movement, Linda Sarsour, so eloquently stated;

> *"....shariah law is reasonable and once you*
> *read into the details it makes a lot of sense."*
> *(Linda Sarsour, Twitter, 2011)*

The enemy of my enemy is NOT your friend. Just because Islam hates the Men of the West just as much as the Third Wave feminist and the progressive socialist Democrats, does not make them a friend or partner. It makes them an ally. Western Men once made a bargain with the devil as well. Only in our case, had it not been for treason the Soviets would have simply imploded after WW2 instead of becoming our greatest threat. The Third Wave and its puppet masters in the socialist wing of the progressive movement have at last shown their intentions. They march around today waving signs decrying borders and travel bans, declaring all the world Americans by right. Anti-Constitutional judges are performing a coup against the plenary power of the President and the Constitutionally defined role of the three branches of government. No Western man should think they have taken their eye from the prize. They haven't. They know that they have won. They just don't know what the price of that victory will be. They should have opened a history book.

BRO KEN

PART IV

A Caliphate Inside A Conundrum Wrapped in a Lie

Now we come to the end stages of the most successful Fifth Column in human history. Third Wave feminism, a vehicle for a socialist insurgency, not a movement for women's rights, has succeeded in its mission to separate Western Men from women in such a way that the damage cannot be repaired in the lifetime of any living person. The goals of Marx, Engels and Lenin have borne fruit in the once indomitable Western democracies. A fruit planted, watered and nurtured by women but heavily aided by the very men they so blatantly despise. Third Wave feminism has been the main catalyst for the progressive agenda since Eugene Debs and Victor Berger realized that the authorities wouldn't shoot women in the streets the way they did male socialist rioters in the 1900's.

The strategy of the progressive socialists has been one of the long view insurgent. They patiently built their base of support within the system that Western men designed and slowly turned that system into a relentless indoctrination system using cradle to grave infusions of half truths and outright lies to poison the well. The very foundations of Western civilization are now its greatest enemy. Through the corruption of law, the creation of mandatory indoctrination in the guise of public education, the ruthless enforcement of political correctness, the bastardization of language and the deliberate dismantling of the family structure, the cabal of Third Wave feminism and the progressive socialist wing of the Democrat party has successfully created a multi-generational rift between the sexes and ended the civilizing influence of the family structure. The rift is not complete, no amount of deceit will ever completely defeat a million years of evolutionary biology or ten thousand years of ingrained tradition. It doesn't have to be 100%, history changing events are never sparked by the masses that suffer them, they need only a small percentage to start the fire.

In America, the divorce rate has been as high as 60% in recent years. At the same time the rate of marriages has declined by about 30%. This trend began in the early seventies and began an unprecedented acceleration in the mid nineties, roughly corresponding with the ascension of Third Wave feminism. The trend began to stabilize in the mid to late 00's at around 40% for divorce and a steadily declining rate of new and second marriages.

Why is this important?

Because Western birth rates have dropped below the ability to sustain itself for one. Not only are Western Men no longer creating replacements, they are now two generations behind the curve. Third Wave feminism has convinced women that bearing children serves only to keep women under the thumb of men and that men only want babies to keep women chained to the stove, unable to realize their full potential. Traditional gender roles have been used as a stick against men based on the lie that evolutionary biology is a myth. Despite the obvious lie, women have bought the propaganda, hook line and sinker. In ever growing numbers women are turning away from seeing men as mates and someone who loves them for the long term and have been convinced that their only value lies in their sexual availability. Women have been convinced that marriage and family are no more than slavery and that "riding the carrousel" throughout their marriage and childbearing years is more fulfilling and self affirming than marrying a good man and raising a family. Any quick perusal of a woman's magazine, or the online world shows that this concept has gone mainstream and now is the "norm" amongst the last two generations of women and will likely only accelerate over the next several generations since "mommy and daddy" are now the exception in American homes, replaced by "baby momma and baby daddy" as the most frequent parental identifier. The endless parade of temporary sexual partners is a powerful teaching tool for those women with children. It teaches their offspring the false lesson that men are throwaway distractions and women serve no purpose to them outside the bedroom. That lesson has now been taught across generations, a primary goal of the progressive socialists because a long view strategy requires self fueling societal trends. Men have now been removed from the American family, leaving government as father. And this goal is now complete.

The next goal on the progressive socialist agenda was to finalize the 1970's trend of women as economic entities of their own. By the 2000's the last vestiges of economic dependence of women on men had been largely broken. The Third Wave feminist and progressive alliance had successfully managed to import sufficient numbers of illegal aliens into the country to dilute the lower middle class and much of the remaining middle class' wages to the point of less than subsistence. Along with the deliberate exporting of manufacturing through the democrat sponsored punitive taxation and over regulation of business, the labor/wage dilution finished off the middle class by either eliminating the jobs all together or so lowering the wage through a willful low wage labor glut that the jobs available to most in the rural areas were insufficient to maintain the one income nuclear family. Never think this was not deliberate and long planned. The groundwork for this was laid in the original socialist movement in the late 19th century and early 20th. The body of written work on this plan is exhaustive and thoroughly documented for any who would see it for what it was. In the early days, 1890 and up until right after WW2 they didn't bother to hide socialist ideas the way they did after the ascension of the Soviet Union in the aftermath of the Rosenberg's treason.

Illegal immigration and border security have been political issues since 1960. Western men put a man on the moon in less than a decade, only a deliberate and widespread effort could have stopped the closure of the southern border. At any point up to about 1996 the states themselves could have done so, up until January 2017 the President could have done so and sealing it would take about 12 hours. Border security is part and partial to national security and national security is the sole province of the Executive branch, or it was. It appears that President Trump has now ceded national defense to the judicial branch, a goal long sought by the progressive wing of the Democrat party.

We now have come to the present day. Now we find ourselves at a crossroads, Western Civilization is dying, not in the fires of a nuclear hell but rather in the lingering bitterness of apathetic indifference. For the Men of the West the long slow strangulation has been exhausting. Between the efforts of the feminist/progressive alliance to destroy the family structure and the efforts of government to kill him through endless wars he was not allowed to win, and a court system that relegated Western Man to third class status in his own home the struggle has temporarily sapped him of his strength and the will to resist the tide. The presidential election of 2016 was seen at first as a reawakening of Western Man by many. Only a few months into the new era it has become obvious that it was not. What had been felt to be a beacon of hope to Western civilization has proven itself to be little more than a distraction from the machinations of the enemy.

What has the socialist/feminist cause accomplished?

• Marriage, as the glue that bound families together, has been so corrupted and denigrated that it is no longer the rule, it is the exception.

• The deliberate importation of cheap, illegal labor coupled with the feminist expectation and legal requirement that women be in the workplace in vast numbers has destroyed the labor market.

• Education, both public and even private at the college level, has been nothing more than a state regulated daycare and indoctrination system for fifty years.

• Language has been bastardized by the education system and the progressive courts to the point where mere words are literally considered violent crimes.

• The culture of "Free Love" that came from Alinskey's methods of protest in the 60's has mainstreamed into women "riding the carrousel" and men "spinning plates" as a form of socially accepted hedonism. Rather than the stability and economic strength of marriage and family, society now caters to the amoral spectacle of women as sexually liberated and free from any moral, political, social or economic consequences. At the same time, men remain socially, economically and legally responsible for their actions with them.

• Religion has been outlawed in the public arena. The Christian God is banned from school, the courtroom, the public square and even private property in many places. Islam, oddly enough, must be accommodated in these places at taxpayer expense.

• The progressive scheme of social entitlement has become so fiscally burdensome that industry was deliberately pushed out of the country, further destabilizing the labor market and creating an even greater burden on the American family to pay for the millions of illegal aliens that come in and take the jobs needed by American families.

• The American press, educated and indoctrinated by socialist professors and a life of exposure to the idea of activist reportage, gleefully promote hedonism and socialistic ideas on one hand, while willfully ignoring or outright lying when it is convenient or against the Marxist dogma they willingly promote.

- As was proven during the 2016 campaign, the progressive democrats own the media. Time and again it has been proven that the mainstream American press does not report, it aids, supports and promotes the progressive socialist agenda.

- Bernie sanders, an admitted socialist, came closer to the Presidency in 2016 than any other since Eugene Debs received nearly 1,000,000 votes in the 1920 Presidential election. Had it not been for the collusion of the American media with Hillary Clinton, Sanders may well have been the first Socialist candidate in the race since 1956 and the first ever to run on a major party ticket. A huge percentage of Sanders financial and grassroots support came from different Feminist groups around America.

- The Third Wave feminist movements recent protests and marches have publicly excluded any women's groups that do not support every single aspect of the national charter. Pro-life groups that had before marched in solidarity are no longer allowed. It now promotes the inclusion of Shariah law as a part of its platform and counts as important feminist icons several vocally pro-Islamist speakers.

Third Wave feminism has now allied itself with radical Islam, this shows two things.

First , they realize that they have won the hearts and minds campaign. They no longer need to stay in the shadows. The strident calls for Shariah as a liberation call to women in the West at the recent Women's marches all over America and the other Western democracies, and the wide public support from the Democrat party for them, proves their alliance is not only real, but welcomed in the seats of political power in Washington. The unleashing of this unexpected alliance in the aftermath of the November election is a deliberate shot across the bow of Western men. This was done to show that financial support for their cause now can flow from the nations of Islam in a manner that undermines the remains of Western civilization and comes with a built in army to create a sense of threat to any that would oppose it. That was the idea behind it. That is what the movement wanted as a takeaway for the public to consume.

It also sends a more important message aimed straight at Western Men. The imagery is well crafted and willfully deliberate. The subtext of Shariah as a siren call to Western women as a form of liberty tells Western men that we are considered less than dogs now. The implication of Islam as the defender of Western women is ludicrous on its face and deliberately baiting to men on a psychological level. Western women have rejected Western Men as suitable partners in the family structure but willingly ally with a system that literally treats them worse than the family milk goat.

That subtext has not gone unnoticed.

Second, the not so secret leadership and guiding hand of Third Wave feminism, the progressive wing of the Democrat party, has played its hold card. The courts, long stacked with unelected legislators, has been deployed to perform a coup and reverse a lawful presidential election. In concert with their socialistic allies in the House and Senate, the Judiciary has moved to depose a sitting President in place. Using classified information leaked from operatives inside the intelligence community and committee, Congress has effectively made it impossible for the President to govern. The courts have stripped him of his plenary power to defend the nation, a power solely granted to the president. The Democrats in congress, along with their Republican allies have thwarted the ability to seat a cabinet, leaving governance in the hands of the existing, democrat appointed bureaucrats who have and will continue to refuse to implement the lawful directives of the Executive. The 9th circuit court, in direct contradiction of Constitutional provisions and long settled law, has used campaign rhetoric rather than legal documentation to impose their legislative decisions. There is no basis whatsoever for that decision. It, in fact, contravenes long existing statute that makes campaign rhetoric inadmissible. They have granted legal citizen status to foreign nationals who have never put foot on American soil and stripped the American citizen of his right to vote in doing so. And no one has done a thing to stop it. Nor will they.

There is no reversing the damage done. Multi-generational rifts cannot be repaired, only survived. The economic system has been damaged to the point where even if it could be restored, building the factories that would return the jobs will take decades. The last twelve years have seen an outflow of American capital, primarily to non-western central banks, that dwarfs the entire GDP of the planet for ten years. That alone enslaves the American taxpayer to foreign entities for two generations at the very least.

An entire generation of our young men has been spent fighting a war they were not allowed to win. Many died, many more were wounded and even more are mentally and emotionally wrecked from spending more time in direct combat in a single year than most saw throughout the entire period of WW2.

Men have seen their rights as parents stripped by the courts and many divorced men have no legal right to even see their children, much less teach them how to be men.

Western women have been convinced that their goal in life should be to work, remain single and sleep with as many men as possible before settling down to a childless, loveless existence with some desperate man and a house full of cats where they live in comfy retirement with no responsibility or passion. That one alone should have been a clue for women. Men built computers and spacecraft, we aren't stupid.

The family is broken. Single parent households are now the rule, not the exception.

America now has millions of disaffected, economically ravaged, childless, unmarried and hopeless men. America has millions more young men without fathers, being raised by single women and the state with no male role model that didn't come off of Craigslist or Tinder and their sisters are being taught by both example and the state that their worth is only in the workplace or on the sexual carrousel.

That is the unintended consequence of factional dominion. Not that this isn't the result they wanted. It is. Without the family structure there is nothing but service to the state, in their mind. That was the goal. The unintended consequence is the lefts failure to read a history that they had not rewritten in their politically correct hindsight.

Had they bothered to do so, they would found out an inescapable fact of having millions of males with no civilizing factor and no hope. This has happened over and over again throughout written history. The result has been the same in every single instance. Until the last 100 years of the Pax Americanus, governments understood what happens when men have no civilizing factor. Under these conditions, men do not simply bow to fate, it is not in our nature. We build societies, cities and civilizations because we are civilized by women, family and responsibility.

When we no longer have those influences?

Could it be that history teaches us the undeniable nature of Men? It is a lesson that was forgotten, but will very soon be taught again. Men build civilizations when we are civilized. Guess what happens when men have no reason to be civilized?

Made in the USA
Columbia, SC
01 October 2018